·TESCO· COOKERY· COLLECTION·

RICE
AND PASTA

TESCO

Recipes written and developed by Janice Murfitt
Additional assistance from the Tesco Consumer Kitchens

Published exclusively for Tesco Stores Ltd,
Delamare Road, Cheshunt, Herts EN8 9SL
by Cathay Books, 59 Grosvenor Street, London W1

First published 1986

© Cathay Books 1986

ISBN 0 86178 393 X

Printed in Hong Kong

ACKNOWLEDGEMENTS

The publishers would like to thank the following company
for their kindness in providing materials and equipment
used in the photography for this book.

Rosenthal Studios – Linie, 3 Abercorn Trading Estate, Middlx HA0 1BB.

We would also like to thank the following
who were concerned in the preparation of the book.

Series Art Director Pedro Prá-Lopez
Photographer Chris Crofton
Stylist Hilary Guy
Food prepared for photography by Janice Murfitt
Special editorial help Cathy Dunn

CONTENTS

NOTE

Standard spoon measurements are used in all recipes

1 tablespoon (tbls) = one 15 ml spoon
1 teaspoon (tsp) = one 5 ml spoon
All spoon measures are level

All eggs are sized 3 or 4 (standard) unless otherwise stated.

For all recipes, quantities are given in both metric and imperial measures. Follow either set but not a mixture of both, as they are not interchangeable.

Following the success of the first 12 books we produced in the Tesco Cookery Collection, we are delighted to be adding 8 new titles to this exciting series. As before, it is the close contact we have with our customers and the feedback we have had through our Consumer Advisory Kitchens which has helped us to select these latest titles. Each one focuses on an area in which our customers have shown particular interest and contains practical background information on the chosen subject together with a wide selection of carefully tested recipes, each one illustrated in colour.

In *Rice and Pasta*, you'll find general information on these popular foods, together with descriptions which tell you in detail how to recognize the different varieties. We've compiled a wide range of recipes from dinner-party specials to quick snacks which you can concoct in minutes for impromptu entertaining. We've included recipes for the best-known and best-loved dishes – for example Beef Stroganoff and Lasagne – but there are plenty of unusual ones too, such as Pork, Apricot and Nut Pilau and Pasta Twists with Walnut Sauce.
I very much hope you will enjoy looking through the book and trying the recipes. Happy Cooking!

Carey Dennis, senior home economist, Tesco Stores Ltd.

INTRODUCTION

As people travel abroad on holiday and become interested in the food they try, many more are experimenting at home and beginning to eat and enjoy the wide variety of foods now available. Rice and pasta are good examples of this and, whereas not so long ago to serve rice and pasta at a meal was something of a novelty, these days most kitchens have one or the other in the cupboard and they are used regularly.

Both rice and pasta lend themselves to quick, creative cooking and they fit very well into today's healthier style of eating as they are starchy, carbohydrate foods that add bulk to our meals. They contain small amounts of protein and vitamins and the brown and wholewheat varieties also provide a little dietary fibre. Because they are carbohydrate foods, rice and pasta always used to be classed as fattening, but this is not so. They are bulky foods and one generous 4-5 oz (100-125 g) serving of cooked pasta or rice contains less than 200 calories – it is the butter and rich sauces which add the calories!

Rice is available in many varieties, as this book will show. It is grown all over the world and is an important part of the economy in several of the South-East Asian countries. Surprisingly, the United States of America has become one of the largest producers in recent years and American Long Grain Rice is now a familiar sight on our supermarket shelves.

In the ancient countries where rice is grown it has become a part of their history and traditions. In Java a girl is not considered eligible for marriage until she can make a perfect bowl of rice!

Cooking rice is one of the skills that many people think they will never master. Our book will help you to learn, but will also introduce you to the different types of rice and the techniques to use when preparing them. Cooking the wonderfully delicate Basmati rice with its delicious nutty flavour is slightly different to the method used for ordinary long grain rice. Cooking brown rice is different again because with its extra bran it takes longer and is much more chewy. All the methods are fully explained in the recipes and there are a whole range to try.

Pasta originated in Italy and is considered one of the most important parts of the meal. In peasant areas where money was short and there was not much meat available, pasta was traditionally used to add bulk to the meal and fill people up. This style of eating, using bulky, carbohydrate foods with vegetables and well-flavoured sauces, combined with only small amounts of fish and meat, is in keeping with the healthier trends of today.

The basis of most pasta is a dough made from a special high protein variety of wheat. This is usually produced plain, but may be enriched with egg or spinach powder to add colour and flavour.

Pasta is either made in a sheet or extruded through a die to make any number of different shapes. It is this that makes it such fun to cook with because every meal can look completely different.

The recipes in this book have been divided into two sections – one for rice and one for pasta. The ideas are interesting and quite straightforward and the photographs will help you to visualise the finished dish.

5

COOKING WITH RICE

The variety that rice offers both in terms of colour, flavour and texture gives plenty of scope to the interested cook. Here is a brief description of each of the different types.

Long-grain rice

The white rice referred to as long-grain rice is usually either Patna or American long-grain which has been milled and polished. When correctly cooked, long-grain rice is fluffy and separates easily, forming an ideal accompaniment to casseroles, Far Eastern dishes, curries or meats and vegetables served with sauces. It also forms the basis for rice dishes such as risottos, pilafs and paellas. Cooked rice can be stir-fried with vegetables or used as a basis for various salads and buffet dishes.

There are several techniques for cooking long-grain rice depending on how you wish to use it, and the recipes provided explain these methods.

Easy-cook rice

This is a 'converted' or pre-fluffed long-grain rice which has been treated with steam under pressure before the milling process. As well as making rice easier to cook successfully, fewer nutrients are lost. It is, however, more expensive than regular long-grain rice. Easy-cook rice can be used in all recipes requiring long-grain rice. Cook as directed on the pack and use as an accompaniment to meat and fish dishes.

Instant or minute rice

This is a long-grain rice which has been pre-cooked then dehydrated. It only requires about 5 minutes cooking time or as directed on the pack. Boil-in-the-bag rice is also quick and easy to use.

Basmati rice

Mainly grown in the upland areas of India and Pakistan, Basmati rice is the finest type of white long-grain rice. Its slender grains are deliciously tender and have a delicate aroma

1 In dish Plain cooked easy-cook rice and cooked Tesco 'Savoury Rice, mixed vegetable flavour – long grain'. **On shelf** Uncooked easy-cook rice

2 In dish Plain cooked brown rice and brown rice cooked with mixed herbs (see Buttered herb rice p 10); **On shelf** Uncooked brown rice

3 In dish Plain cooked Basmati rice and Basmati cooked with turmeric; **On shelf** Uncooked Basmati rice

4 In dish Plain cooked long-grain rice and long-grain rice cooked with tomato (see Tomato rice p 12); **On shelf** Uncooked long-grain rice

and faintly nutty taste. It requires careful cooking but it is well worth trying. Cook as directed on the pack or use the method outlined on page 12.

Brown rice

This is the most natural of all types of rice with only the outer husks removed. The high-fibre bran is retained along with vitamins and minerals. It takes longer to cook than regular white rice but has a firm texture and a pleasant nutty flavour which makes it an attractive alternative to Patna or American rice.

To prepare, follow the directions on the pack or refer to the method given on page 28. Brown rice makes a substantial accompaniment to vegetable dishes and is a good stuffing ingredient for fish, meat and whole vegetables.

Short and medium-grained rice

These types of rice are plumper with a higher starch content than regular long-grain rice. Varieties such as the medium-grained Carolina and Spanish or Italian rice can be used for savoury dishes such as risottos and paellas but are particularly good for puddings where the grains are required to absorb a large amount of liquid.

The thick, short-grained white rice is excellent for puddings and desserts and gives a creamy-rich texture. It requires a long, slow cooking method and is usually baked in the oven. In Italy, savoury risottos are made with short-grained rice of a special kind called Arborio

Ground rice

Ground rice is used for various baked puddings, moulds and other desserts. It is, in fact a ground-up rice, with the texture of flour. It can be used in baking mixed with wheat flour for biscuits and cakes and is sometimes used for thickening soups.

Wild rice

Strictly-speaking, this is not a true rice, but the seed of a wild grass which grows along the lake shores in northern USA and parts of Canada. It is regarded as a delicacy and is expensive to buy because it has to be harvested by hand. Wild rice has an unusual nutty flavour and chewy texture and requires a longer cooking time.

To cook wild rice, follow the directions on the pack or use the method outlined for brown rice. Wild rice is particularly good served with sliced mushrooms which have been simmered in a little butter and sherry and garnished with fresh chives.

1

1 In dish Plain cooked Uncle Ben's Long grain and Wild Rice mix and cooked Uncle Ben's Long-grain and Wild Rice mix with red and yellow peppers; **On shelf** Easy-cook rice and wild rice

2 In dish Cooked plain instant rice and cooked instant rice with fried bacon, onion and mushrooms; **On shelf** Uncooked instant rice

3 In dish Cooked plain ground rice and cooked ground rice with grated nutmeg; **On shelf** Uncooked ground rice

4 In dish Plain boiled pudding rice and cooked rice pudding; **On shelf** Uncooked short-grain pudding rice and uncooked small grain Arborio

4

2

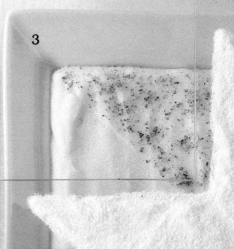

3

Buttered herbed rice

SERVES 4

1.2 litres (2 pints) water
1 tsp salt
225 g (8 oz) long-grain rice
50 g (2 oz) butter
1 tsp chopped fresh coriander
1 tsp chopped fresh parsley
1 tsp chopped fresh basil
fresh coriander leaves, to garnish

Place water and salt in a large saucepan and bring to the boil, add the rice and stir well.

Reduce the heat, cover the saucepan with a lid and simmer for 10 minutes until grains are almost tender.

Pour the rice into a sieve, rinse with hot water and drain well.

Rinse out the saucepan, add the butter and heat until melted. Add the herbs and rice and stir until well blended. Place in a warmed serving dish and garnish with a few fresh coriander leaves.

Serving idea: Serve with any meat dishes, especially casseroles or fish dishes with a sauce.

Variation: Try a variety of different freshly chopped herbs such as thyme, rosemary, marjoram, sage.

• Buttered herbed rice; Fried rice; Crispy rice

Fried rice

SERVES 4

750 ml (1¼ pints) water
1 tsp salt
225 g (8 oz) brown rice
25 g (1 oz) butter or margarine
2 eggs, beaten
pepper
chopped fresh parsley, to garnish

Place the water and salt in a large saucepan and bring to the boil, add the rice and stir well.

Reduce the heat and cover the saucepan with a lid and simmer for 30 minutes until the grains are almost tender.

Pour the rice into a sieve and rinse with hot water and drain well.

Rinse out the saucepan, add the butter or margarine and heat until melted. Add the rice, stir lightly with a fork and fry for 3 minutes.

Stir in the beaten eggs and pepper and cook for 1 minute until the egg looks scrambled. Place on a warmed serving dish and sprinkle with chopped parsley.

Serving idea: Serve with oriental dishes such as stir-fried vegetables or with Middle Eastern dishes like kebabs.

Crispy rice

SERVES 4

225 g (8 oz) long-grain rice
1 tsp salt
water
50 g (2 oz) butter or margarine
¼ tsp saffron threads or ½ tsp
  turmeric

Place the rice, salt and enough water to cover the rice in a saucepan. Bring to the boil and cook for 5 minutes. Pour the rice into a sieve and drain well.

Rinse out the saucepan, add the butter, saffron and 4 tbls water. Bring to the boil and pour half the liquid into a cup.

Add the rice to the saucepan and stir, then press down well to make level. Make a hole in the centre of the rice with a wooden spoon handle so the steam can circulate. Cover with a lid and cook over a moderate heat for 5 minutes.

Pour the remaining liquid over the surface of the rice and cover with a lid. Cook on a low heat for 40 minutes until a golden crust has formed on the base and the rice on top is just tender.

Leave to stand for 5 minutes. Spoon the soft rice onto a warmed serving dish and place the crispy layer on top.

Serving idea: Serve with grilled meats or kebabs, or soft food for added texture.

Variation: Turn this recipe into a main dish by adding cooked, diced meat and vegetables to the rice.

Coconut rice

SERVES 4

600 ml (1 pint) water
1 tsp salt
100 g (4 oz) creamed coconut
225 g (8 oz) easy-cook rice
2 tbls desiccated coconut
sprig of fresh coriander, to garnish

Place the water, salt and creamed coconut in a medium saucepan and bring to the boil. Stir occasionally until the coconut has melted. Stir in the rice.

Reduce the heat, cover the saucepan with a lid and simmer for 12-15 minutes until almost all the liquid has been absorbed.

Stir gently with a fork and add a little more water if the grains are too sticky.

Place the rice in a warmed serving dish and sprinkle with the coconut which has been lightly toasted under a moderate grill for 2-3 minutes. Garnish with a sprig of fresh coriander. Serve with curried or spicy meat, fish or vegetable dishes.

Sweet pilau rice

SERVES 4

600 ml (1 pint) water
1 tsp salt
½ tsp turmeric
4 cardamom pods, split
4 cloves
2.5 cm (1 inch) stick cinnamon
225 g (8 oz) short-grain or easy-cook rice
50 g (2 oz) seedless raisins
1 red pepper, seeded and finely chopped
100 g (4 oz) frozen peas
40 g (1½ oz) flaked almonds

Place the water, salt, turmeric, cardamom pods, cloves and cinnamon stick in a medium saucepan and bring to the boil. Stir the rice and raisins into the water.

Reduce the heat, cover the saucepan with a lid and simmer for 10 minutes until most of the liquid has been absorbed by the rice. Remove the cinnamon stick.

Gently stir in the pepper and peas, using a fork. Cover and cook for a further 3 minutes.

Toast the almonds under a medium grill until golden brown.

Stir half the almonds into the rice and place in a warmed serving dish. Scatter remaining almonds on top.

Tomato rice

SERVES 4

1.2 litres (2 pints) water
1 tsp salt
225 g (8 oz) Basmati or long-grain rice
1 tbls vegetable oil
1 onion, finely chopped
1 clove garlic, crushed
4-5 large tomatoes, skinned, seeded and chopped
1 tbls chopped fresh basil or ½ tbls dried basil
cayenne pepper
fresh basil leaves, to garnish

Place the water and salt in a large saucepan and bring to the boil, add the rice and stir well.

Reduce the heat, cover the saucepan with a lid and simmer for 10 minutes until the grains are almost tender.

Pour the rice into a sieve, rinse with hot water and drain well.

Rinse out the saucepan, and heat the oil. Stir in the onion and garlic and cook gently for 2-3 minutes until tender.

Add the tomatoes, basil and cayenne pepper and cook for 1 minute, then add the rice and stir gently with a fork until well mixed.

Place the rice on a warmed serving dish. Garnish with fresh basil leaves.

● From top: Sweet pilau rice; Coconut rice; Tomato rice

Beef stroganoff

SERVES 4

2 tbls vegetable oil
1 onion, thinly sliced
225 g (8 oz) button mushrooms
450 g (1 lb) fillet steak, in thin strips
1 tsp mustard powder
1 tsp soft brown sugar
1 tbls tomato purée
3 tbls dry sherry
salt and pepper
142 ml (5 fl oz) carton soured cream
fresh bay leaves or parsley, to
    garnish

Heat the oil in a large frying pan. Add the onion and mushrooms and cook for 4-5 minutes or until tender. Remove from the frying pan using a slotted spoon and place on a plate.

Add the steak and fry quickly for 1 minute. Mix together in a bowl the mustard, sugar, tomato purée, sherry and salt and pepper. Pour over the meat, stir well and bring to the boil.

Add the mushrooms and onions and stir occasionally until heated through. Remove the frying pan from the heat and stir in the soured cream.

Place on a warmed serving dish

and garnish with fresh bay leaves or parsley.

Serving idea: Serve with buttered herbed rice and a green salad.

Variation: Replace the steak with pork fillet or chicken or turkey breasts cut into strips.

Note: This is a classic dish to serve with rice or tagliatelle. It can be made in advance and frozen for up to one month without the soured cream.

• Left to right: Beef stroganoff; Spicy chicken pilaf

Spicy chicken pilaf

SERVES 4

1 ¼ kg (2½ lb) chicken
2 tbls plain flour
1 tsp allspice
¼ tsp grated nutmeg
3 cloves, crushed
salt and pepper
2 tbls vegetable oil
4 streaky bacon rashers, rinded, boned and chopped
1 onion, chopped
100 g (4 oz) button mushrooms, sliced
225 g (8 oz) short-grain rice
600 ml (1 pint) chicken stock
50 g (2 oz) sultanas
1 tsp salt
1 green pepper, seeded and chopped
100 g (4 oz) sweetcorn kernels
lemon twists and parsley, to garnish

Cut the legs and wings off the chicken and remove the skin. Take all the flesh off the bones and cut into bite-sized pieces.

Place the flour, allspice, nutmeg, cloves and salt and pepper in a polythene bag. Add the chicken pieces and toss to coat evenly.

Fry the bacon in a medium saucepan for 2-3 minutes until crisp. Add the onion, mushrooms and rice and fry for 3 minutes.

Stir in the stock, sultanas and 1 tsp salt. Bring to the boil, then reduce the heat and cover with a lid.

Simmer for 10 minutes until the rice is almost tender. Stir in the pepper and sweetcorn with a fork, cover and cook for 2 minutes, then remove from the heat.

Heat the remaining oil in a frying pan, add the chicken and cook for 3-4 minutes until tender.

Stir the chicken into the rice and place on a warmed serving dish. Garnish with lemon and parsley and serve with a salad of radicchio, cucumber and watercress.

• Pork, apricot and nut pilau; Liver and orange pilau

Liver and orange pilau

SERVES 4

2 tbls vegetable oil
4 streaky bacon rashers, rinded,
  boned and chopped
1 onion, chopped
4 fresh sage leaves or 1 tsp dried
  sage
pepper
225 g (8 oz) long-grain rice
750 ml (1¼ pints) vegetable stock
  or water
2 oranges
15 g (½ oz) butter, melted
12 pickling onions, peeled
100 g (4 oz) button mushrooms,
  quartered
275 g (10 oz) lambs' liver, cut into
  thin strips
2 tbls plain flour

Fry half the bacon with 1 tbls of the oil in a medium saucepan for 2 minutes. Add the onion, 2 sage leaves, pepper and rice, stir well and cook for 3 minutes.

Add 600 ml (1 pint) stock and bring to the boil, stirring. Reduce the heat and cover the saucepan with a lid.

Simmer for 10 minutes until the grains are almost tender, then turn off the heat.

Grate the rind from one orange and use a sharp knife to peel the pith away from the flesh. Cut the orange into segments and chop, then stir gently into the rice mixture with the rind.

Pile the rice into a serving dish or casserole and keep warm while preparing the liver and orange mixture.

Pork, apricot and nut pilau

SERVES 4

3 tbls sunflower or sesame seed oil
2 tbls white wine vinegar
1 clove garlic, crushed
1 tsp chopped fresh coriander or
    flat-leaved parsley
1 tsp chopped fresh fennel or 6
    dried fennel seeds
salt and pepper
450 g (1 lb) pork fillet, trimmed of
    all fat and cut into bite-sized
    pieces
1 onion, chopped
100 g (4 oz) dried apricots, chopped
225 g (8 oz) brown rice
600 ml (1 pint) chicken or vegetable
    stock
100 g (4 oz) French beans, chopped
40 g (1½ oz) flaked almonds
To garnish:
4 apricot halves
sprigs of fresh coriander and fennel

Heat the remaining oil in a frying pan, add the remaining bacon and pickling onions and cook for 4 minutes.

Add the mushrooms and liver and fry quickly for 2 minutes. Stir in the flour and cook for 1 minute.

Add the remaining stock, stir well, bring to the boil and cook for 1 minute.

Cut 4 orange slices from the remaining orange for garnish and squeeze the juice from the rest and stir into the liver mixture.

When thoroughly heated, pour the liver mixture over the warm rice in the serving dish. Garnish with orange slices and the remaining sage leaves.

Serving idea: Serve with grilled tomatoes and buttered courgettes.

Variations: Replace the liver with 10 lambs' kidneys.

Mix together in a bowl the oil, vinegar, garlic, coriander or parsley, fennel, salt and pepper. Add the meat and stir well. Cover with cling film and leave in a cool place for several hours or overnight.

Strain the marinade into a medium saucepan and heat. Add the onion, apricots and rice and cook for 3 minutes.

Stir in the stock, bring to the boil, then reduce the heat and cover the saucepan with a lid.

Simmer for 30 minutes until the rice is almost tender. Add the beans and cook for 6-8 minutes, then turn off the heat.

Place the meat in a frying pan and cook quickly for 3-4 minutes.

Arrange the rice on a warmed serving plate and sprinkle with almonds which have been toasted under a medium grill until golden brown. Pile the meat on top and garnish with apricots and fresh herbs. Serve with freshly cooked vegetables in season.

Rice medley layer

SERVES 4

1 litre (1¾ pts) chicken stock
salt and pepper
½ tsp turmeric
350 g (12 oz) long-grain rice
50 g (2 oz) butter or margarine
1 onion, chopped
4 tomatoes, skinned, seeded,
* chopped*
1 tbls tomato purée
¼ tsp dried mixed herbs
1 tsp caster sugar
2 streaky bacon rashers, rinded,
* boned and chopped*
50 g (2 oz) button mushrooms,
* chopped*
275 g (10 oz) turkey fillet, chopped
2 courgettes, sliced
To garnish:
sprigs of parsley
courgette, mushroom and tomato
* slices*

Heat the oven to 190°C, 375°F, Gas Mark 5. Place half the stock, 1 tsp salt and the turmeric in a large saucepan and bring to the boil.

Stir in the rice, then reduce the heat and cover the saucepan with a lid. Cook for 8-10 minutes until the stock has been absorbed.

Melt 25 g (1 oz) butter in a frying pan and stir in the onion, tomatoes, tomato purée, salt and pepper, herbs and sugar.

Cook for 5 minutes until the mixture is thick and all the liquid has evaporated.

Butter a 20 cm (8 inch) soufflé dish or a cake tin and line the base with greaseproof paper.

Spread one third of the rice over the base and cover with the tomato mixture. Spread with another third of the rice.

Melt the remaining butter in the frying pan and add the bacon, mushrooms, turkey and some salt and pepper. Fry quickly for 1 minute, stirring continuously.

Arrange half of the courgette slices over the rice and spread with the turkey mixture. Top with remaining courgettes and rice and press well down.

Pour the remaining stock over the rice mixture and cover with a piece of buttered foil.

Cook in the centre of the oven for 30-35 minutes or until the rice is tender.

Cool in the dish for 5 minutes, then invert onto a warmed serving dish. Carefully remove the cooking dish and paper.

Garnish with sprigs of parsley, courgette, mushrooms and tomato slices.

● **Yoghurt lime lamb with saffron rice; Rice medley layer**

Yoghurt lime lamb with saffron rice

SERVES 4

150 g (5.29 oz) carton natural
  yoghurt
2 tsp clear honey
1 tbls grated fresh ginger
1 garlic clove, crushed
1 lime, grated rind and 1 tbls juice
450 g (1 lb) neck fillet of lamb, cut
  into cubes
600 ml (1 pint) water
1 tsp salt
1/4 tsp saffron threads or a few
  grains of saffron powder
225 g (8 oz) Basmati rice
To garnish:
fresh mint leaves
wedges of lime and grated rind

Place the yoghurt, honey, ginger, garlic, lime rind and juice in a bowl and mix well together.

Add the lamb and stir until evenly coated. Cover with cling film and leave for several hours or overnight.

Place the water, salt and saffron in a medium saucepan and bring to the boil. Stir in the rice then reduce the heat and cover the saucepan with a lid. Simmer for 10 minutes, until all the liquid has been absorbed and the grains are tender.

Using a slotted spoon remove the lamb from the marinade and place it in a grill pan. Cook under a high heat for 5 minutes, turning only once and basting with the marinade during the cooking. Serve with rice, garnished with mint, lime wedges and rind.

Savoury rice dolmades

MAKES ABOUT 40

1 tbls olive oil
1 onion, chopped
350 g (12 oz) minced beef
2 tbls chopped fresh celery leaves
1 garlic clove, crushed
2 tsp tomato purée
salt and pepper
225 g (8 oz) brown rice
600 ml (1 pint) beef or vegetable
    stock
227 g (8 oz) packet vine leaves in
    brine
6 tomatoes, skinned and chopped

Heat the oil in a saucepan and add the onion, minced beef, celery leaves, garlic, tomato purée, salt, pepper and rice. Stir well and cook quickly to brown the meat.

Add the stock and bring to the boil, then reduce the heat and cover the saucepan with a lid.

Simmer for 25 minutes until all the liquid has been absorbed and the grains are almost tender. Remove saucepan from heat and leave until mixture is cool.

Drain the vine leaves and place in a bowl, cover with boiling water and leave for 15 minutes, then drain and rinse in cold water.

Take a few leaves and use to line the base of a medium saucepan. Add a ¼ pt of water.

Place a vine leaf on a board and spoon on a little of the rice mixture in the centre. Fold the sides of the leaf into the centre and roll up firmly.

Repeat to fill all the leaves, then pack tightly in the saucepan. Top with chopped tomatoes and place a plate on top to keep the dolmades in place.

Cover the saucepan with a lid and cook gently for 40 minutes, adding a little more water if necessary.

Arrange the dolmades on a warmed serving dish and spoon the tomato mixture on top.

Serving idea: Serve warm or cold with pitta bread and salad.

Curried chicken and rice ring

SERVES 4

1.2 litres (2 pints) water
1 tsp salt
225 g (8 oz) easy-cook rice
200 ml (⅓ pint) thick mayonnaise
4 tbls natural yoghurt
2-3 tsp medium-strength curry
    paste
2 tsp mango chutney
salt and pepper
1 tbls chopped fresh coriander
    leaves
450 g (1 lb) cooked chicken, cut into
    bite-sized pieces
To garnish:
radicchio leaves
sprigs of watercress
cucumber slices
lemon slices

Place the water and salt in a saucepan and bring to the boil. Add the rice then reduce the heat and cover the saucepan with a lid.

Simmer for 10 minutes until the grains are almost tender, then pour the rice into a sieve and rinse with cold water. Leave until cold.

Place the mayonnaise, yoghurt, curry paste, chutney, salt, pepper and coriander in a bowl. Mix together until well blended.

Stir in the chicken and rice and mix well together. Press the mixture into a 20 cm (8 inch) plain ring mould, which has been rinsed in cold water and shaken to remove excess water, then invert onto a serving dish and garnish.

• From top: Curried chicken and rice ring; Savoury rice dolmades

---

Seafood risotto

SERVES 4

50 g (2 oz) butter or margarine
1 onion, chopped
1 yellow pepper, seeded and
  chopped
1 red pepper, seeded and chopped
4 tomatoes, skinned, seeded and
  chopped
225 g (8 oz) cod fillet, skinned
6 scallops, cleaned
salt and pepper
225 g (8 oz) easy-cook or Italian
  short-grain rice
600 ml (1 pint) vegetable stock or
  water
175 g (6 oz) smoked mackerel fillet,
  skinned
2 tbls grated Parmesan cheese
1 tbls chopped fresh parsley and
  parsley sprigs

Melt 25 g (1 oz) of butter or margarine in a medium saucepan, add the onion, peppers and tomatoes. Cook for 1 minute, stirring occasionally.

Cut the fish into bite-sized pieces. Add the cod and scallops to the tomato mixture with some salt and pepper and cook for 3 minutes. Pour the fish mixture into a bowl.

Melt remaining butter in the pan, add rice and fry for 3 minutes.

Stir in the stock or water and 1 tsp salt and bring to the boil. Then reduce the heat and cover the saucepan with a lid. Cook gently for 10 minutes until the liquid has been absorbed and the grains are almost tender.

Add the fish mixture and mackerel and stir gently to mix evenly.

Heat the risotto for 2 minutes until hot and creamy in texture. Serve with Parmesan cheese and parsley.

Paella

SERVES 4

2 chicken leg joints
2 tbls olive oil
1 large onion, sliced
1 red pepper, seeded and sliced
4 tomatoes, skinned, seeded and
  chopped
1 garlic clove, crushed
50 g (2 oz) boneless pork, chopped
225 g (8 oz) long-grain rice
1/4 tsp powdered saffron or turmeric
1 tsp salt
pepper
600 ml (1 pint) chicken stock
8 mussels in shells, scrubbed
12 whole prawns, washed
100 g (4 oz) piece garlic sausage
50 g (2 oz) frozen peas
1 lemon cut into wedges, to serve

Cut each chicken leg in half through the joint to make 2 drumsticks and 2 thigh joints.

Heat 1 tbls oil in a large frying pan until very hot. Quickly fry the chicken joints until evenly browned all over. Place the joints on a plate.

Wipe out the frying pan with absorbent paper and heat the remainder of the oil.

Add the onion, pepper, tomatoes, garlic and pork, stir well and cook for about 8-10 minutes until the mixture has thickened and no moisture remains.

Stir in the rice, saffron, salt and pepper and cook for 3 minutes, then stir in the stock and bring the mixture slowly to the boil.

Remove the beard or black string-like tufts from the mussels and remove the legs and any eggs from the prawns.

Stir the rice mixture with a fork gently to mix well, then arrange the chicken joints, mussels in their shells, prawns, chopped sausage and peas on top of the rice.

Cover the frying pan with a lid and cook gently for 15-20 minutes until almost all the liquid has been absorbed and the rice grains are tender.

Serving idea: Serve straight from the pan with wedges of lemon.

● Seafood risotto; Paella

Stuffed plaice on tomato rice

SERVES 4

4 plaice fillets, skinned
150 g (5.29 oz) carton natural
  yoghurt
½ tsp cayenne pepper
For the tomato rice:
400 g (14 oz) can chopped tomatoes
1 tsp salt
1 tsp sugar
1 bay leaf
225 g (8 oz) easy-cook rice
For the stuffing and topping:
25 g (1 oz) butter or margarine
3 spring onions, chopped
50 g (2 oz) button mushrooms,
  chopped
50 g (2 oz) peeled prawns
1 tbls chopped fresh chervil or
  ½ tbls dried chervil
2 tbls fresh white breadcrumbs
salt and pepper
fresh chervil, lemon twists and
  prawns, to garnish

Heat the oven to 190°C, 375°F, Gas Mark 5. For the tomato rice, place the tomatoes, salt, sugar and bay leaf in a medium saucepan. Stir in the rice and reduce the heat. Cover and cook gently for 10 minutes.

Melt the butter or margarine in a small frying pan, add the onions and mushrooms. Cook until tender.

Stir in the prawns, chervil, breadcrumbs and some salt and pepper. Place some stuffing in the middle of each fillet and then fold each fish fillet in half.

Pour the rice mixture into a shallow ovenproof dish and arrange the fish fillets on top.

Mix the yoghurt and cayenne pepper together and spoon over the fish to coat evenly. Cover the dish with a piece of buttered foil and cook in the centre of the oven for 20 minutes, or until the rice and fish are tender.

Garnish with fresh chervil, lemon twists and prawns; serve with green beans and sweetcorn.

● From top: Stuffed plaice with tomato rice; Tuna fish and fennel risotto; Kedgeree

Tuna fish and fennel risotto

SERVES 4

1 tbls vegetable oil
1 onion, chopped
2 streaky bacon rashers, rinded,
  boned and chopped
1 fennel bulb, chopped
100 g (4 oz) button mushrooms,
  sliced
225 g (8 oz) long-grain rice
397 g (14 oz) can chopped tomatoes
2 tsp tomato purée
300 ml (½ pint) vegetable stock or
  water
grated rind of 1 lemon
1 tbls lemon juice
few drops Tabasco sauce
salt and pepper
198 g (7 oz) can tuna in oil, drained
50 g (2 oz) frozen peas
1 tbls grated Parmesan cheese
fresh fennel leaves and slices to
  garnish

Heat the oil in a medium saucepan. Add the onion, bacon and fennel and cook for 2 minutes until tender.

Stir in the mushrooms and rice and cook for 3 minutes. Add the tomatoes, tomato purée, stock, lemon rind and juice, Tabasco sauce, salt and pepper.

Bring to the boil, stirring, then reduce the heat and cover the saucepan with a lid. Cook gently for 5 minutes.

Flake the tuna with a fork and add it to the rice mixture with the peas. Continue cooking for 5-8 minutes until most of the liquid has been absorbed and the rice grains are tender.

Place the risotto in a warmed serving dish, sprinkle with Parmesan cheese and garnish with fennel leaves and slices.

Kedgeree

SERVES 4

900 ml (1½ pints) water
1 tsp salt
225 g (8 oz) brown rice
50 g (2 oz) butter
1 onion, chopped
275 g (10 oz) smoked haddock,
cooked and flaked (see note
below)
3 hard-boiled eggs, shelled and
chopped
pepper
2 tbls double cream
1 tbls chopped fresh parsley
parsley sprigs
egg slices

Place the water and salt in a medium saucepan and bring to the boil. Stir in the rice, then reduce the heat and cover the saucepan with a lid. Cook very gently for 20-25 minutes until the rice grains are tender.

Pour the rice into a sieve and rinse with hot water, then drain well.

Rinse out the saucepan, and heat the butter until melted. Stir in the onion and cook gently for 2-3 minutes until tender.

Stir in the fish, egg, some pepper and the rice. Heat gently for 1-2 minutes, then remove the saucepan from the heat.

Add the cream, mix together lightly and place on a warmed serving dish. Garnish with slices of egg, chopped parsley and parsley sprigs.

Note: To cook fish, poach in simmering water for 5-6 minutes or until the fish is just tender.

Fish and rice soup

SERVES 4

25 g (1 oz) butter or margarine
1 onion, chopped
50 g (2 oz) bulb fennel, chopped
100 g (4 oz) cucumber, seeded and
  chopped
2 tomatoes, skinned, seeded and
  chopped
75 g (3 oz) Basmati rice
1.2 litres (2 pints) vegetable stock or
  water
salt and pepper
225 g (8 oz) piece of skate
225 g (8 oz) piece of monkfish
chopped fresh fennel leaves, to
  garnish

Melt the butter or margarine in a
large saucepan. Add the onion, fennel and cucumber and cook gently
for 2 minutes until the vegetables
are almost tender.

• Fish and rice soup

Stir in the tomatoes and rice and
cook for 3 minutes. Add the stock,
salt and pepper and bring the
soup mixture to the boil, stirring
occasionally.

Place the whole pieces of fish into
the soup. Reduce the heat and cover
the saucepan with a lid.

Cook gently for 20 minutes until
the rice is tender, then remove the
fish.

Remove the skin and bones from
the fish and flake the flesh, then
return to the soup.

Serve hot in small bowls sprinkled
with fennel leaves.

Serving idea: Serve the soup with
warm, crusty rolls and butter.

Variation: Replace the fish with any
variety of your choice.

Cheesy oven risotto

SERVES 4

50 g (2 oz) vegetable margarine
2 leeks, sliced
100 g (4 oz) green beans, chopped
1 red pepper, seeded and chopped
1 yellow pepper, seeded and
   chopped
175 g (6 oz) button mushrooms,
   sliced
225 g (8 oz) short-grain rice
600 ml (1 pint) vegetable stock
salt and pepper
100 g (4 oz) Cheddar cheese,
   grated
1 sprig fresh parsley

Heat the oven to 190°C, 375°F, Gas Mark 5. Melt the margarine in a medium saucepan.

Add the leeks, beans, peppers and mushrooms and cook for 2 minutes, stirring occasionally. Stir in the rice and cook for 3 minutes.

Add the stock, ½ tsp salt and some pepper and bring to the boil.

Pour the risotto mixture into a 1½ litre (3 pint) casserole dish and cover with a lid or foil.

Cook in the centre of the oven for 30 minutes or until most of the stock has been absorbed and the grains are tender.

Remove the lid, stir the risotto, sprinkle with the cheese and cook, uncovered, for a further 3 minutes until the cheese has melted.

Serve immediately garnished with a parsley sprig.

● **Cheesy oven risotto**

• Brown rice salad; Tropical rice salad

Brown rice salad

SERVES 4

750 ml (1¼ pints) water
salt
225 g (8 oz) brown rice
198 g (7 oz) can red kidney beans,
*   rinsed and drained*
198 g (7 oz) can sweetcorn, drained
340 g (12 oz) can flageolet beans,
*   drained*
radicchio or lettuce leaves
100 g (4 oz) Feta cheese, chopped
100 g (4 oz) Edam cheese, rinded
*   and sliced*
For the dressing:
2 tbls olive oil
1 tbls tarragon vinegar
1 tsp clear honey
½ garlic clove, crushed
salt and pepper
sprigs of watercress, to garnish

Place the water and 1 tsp salt in a medium saucepan and bring to the boil. Stir in the rice, then reduce the heat and cover the saucepan with a lid.

Cook gently for 35 minutes until all the water has been absorbed and the rice grains are almost tender.

Pour the rice into a sieve and rinse under cold water, then drain thoroughly and place in a bowl.

Add the kidney beans, sweetcorn and flageolet beans to the rice. Stir gently to mix well.

Place the dressing ingredients in a bowl. Whisk well until thoroughly blended, then pour over the rice mixture and stir.

Arrange radicchio leaves on a serving dish and spread the rice salad over. Arrange lines of Feta and Edam cheese over the rice and garnish with sprigs of watercress.

Tropical rice salad

SERVES 4-6

600 ml (1 pint) water
salt
225 g (8 oz) easy-cook rice
1 small or ½ medium fresh
  pineapple
1 red pepper, seeded and chopped
1 fennel bulb, chopped
100 g (4 oz) celeriac, grated
1 kiwi fruit, peeled and chopped
2 tbls pumpkin seeds
fennel leaves, to garnish
For the dressing:
2 tbls sunflower seed oil
1 tbls red wine vinegar
¼ tsp made mustard
salt and pepper

Place the water and 1 tsp salt in a medium saucepan and bring to the boil. Stir in the rice then reduce the heat and cover the saucepan.

Cook gently for 15 minutes or until all the water has been absorbed and the grains are almost tender.

Pour the rice into a sieve and rinse under cold water, then drain thoroughly and place in a bowl.

Cut the pineapple in half lengthways and remove the flesh with a serrated knife. Cut out the core and chop the flesh, then place the chopped pineapple in a bowl.

Add the pepper, fennel, celeriac, kiwi fruit and pumpkin seeds to the rice and stir gently to mix well.

Place the dressing ingredients in a bowl. Whisk well until thoroughly blended.

Pour the dressing over the rice mixture and toss well to coat evenly.

Serve in a large bowl with a mixed green salad as an accompaniment. Alternatively, serve on individual plates lined with green salad leaves such as lettuce, chicory or endive. Or serve on its own or with a variety of sliced cheeses.

Coconut rice cakes with vegetable stir-fry

SERVES 4

For the rice cakes:
1 quantity of Coconut rice (see page 12)
25 g (1 oz) vegetable margarine
2 tbls grated onion
40 g (1½ oz) grated Parmesan cheese
40 g (1½ oz) grated Cheddar cheese
salt and pepper
¼ tsp made mustard
1 egg, beaten
sunflower or sesame seed oil
For the stir-fry vegetables:
½ onion, thinly sliced
1 green pepper, seeded, thinly sliced
3 carrots, cut into thin strips
6 Chinese leaves, cut into thin strips
100 g (4 oz) button mushrooms, thinly sliced
175 g (6 oz) fresh bean sprouts
1 tbls light soy sauce
To garnish:
1 tbls sunflower or sesame seeds
carrot slices and chives

Make the Coconut rice according to instructions (page 12). Heat the margarine in a small frying pan, add the onion and cook for 2 minutes or until tender.

Add the onion, Parmesan and Cheddar cheeses, salt, pepper, mustard and egg to the rice mixture and stir until well blended.

Divide the mixture into 4 and shape each into 15 cm (6 inch) rounds.

Heat a little oil in the frying pan, add a rice cake and fry for 2-3 minutes until the underside is golden brown.

Carefully turn the rice cake over and cook the other side until brown.

Drain on absorbent paper, keep warm while frying remaining cakes.

To make the stir-fry vegetables, heat 1 tbls oil in the frying pan. Quickly fry the onion, pepper and carrots, stirring, for 1 minute.

Stir in the Chinese leaves, mushrooms and bean sprouts and cook for 1 minute. Add the soy sauce and some salt and pepper.

Place each rice cake on a warmed serving plate and top with stir-fry vegetables. Sprinkle with sunflower or sesame seeds, and garnish with carrot slices and chives.

Vegetable biryani

SERVES 4

750 ml (1¼ pints) vegetable stock
¼ tsp saffron threads, crushed or ½ tsp turmeric
225 g (8 oz) Basmati rice
175 g (6 oz) potatoes, roughly chopped
2 carrots, sliced
2 tbls ghee or vegetable oil
1 onion, chopped
1 garlic clove, crushed
½ tsp cumin seeds
½ tsp ground coriander
½ tsp turmeric
¼ tsp fennel seeds
salt and pepper
2 courgettes, sliced
2 sticks celery, sliced
100 g (4 oz) French beans, chopped
fresh coriander leaves to garnish

Heat the oven to 190°C, 375°F, Gas Mark 5. Place 300 ml (½ pint) stock and the saffron in a medium saucepan and bring to the boil.

Stir in the rice, then reduce the heat and cover the saucepan with a lid.

Cook gently for 5 minutes until all the liquid has been absorbed and place the rice in a bowl.

• From top: Vegetable biryani; Coconut rice cakes with vegetable stir-fry

Place the remaining stock in the saucepan, bring to the boil, add the potatoes and carrots and cook for 4 minutes or until the vegetables are tender, then remove with a slotted spoon, reserving the stock.

Heat the ghee in a large frying pan. Stir in the onion, garlic, cumin, coriander, turmeric, fennel, salt and pepper and cook gently for 5 minutes.

Add the potatoes, carrots, courgettes, celery and beans and cook for 2 minutes, stirring occasionally.

Spread half the rice over the base of a 2.4 litre (4 pint) casserole dish, then cover the rice with the vegetable mixture.

Cover the vegetables with the remaining rice and pour over the stock.

Cover with a lid or foil and cook in the oven for 30 minutes or until the rice grains are tender. Mix gently together with a fork and serve with fresh coriander leaves.

Rice croquettes with spicy sauce

MAKES ABOUT 20

These little croquettes make ideal dinner party starters or buffet eats. You can prepare the croquettes in advance and keep them for a day in the refrigerator before cooking.

For the croquettes:
25 g (1 oz) vegetable margarine
1 onion, chopped
225 g (8 oz) short-grain rice
600 ml (1 pint) vegetable stock
1 tsp salt
pepper
20 tiny button mushrooms
100 g (4 oz) St Paulin cheese, cubed
3 eggs, beaten
75 g (3 oz) fresh white breadcrumbs
oil for deep frying
sprigs of parsley and lemon wedges, to garnish
For the sauce:
1 tbls vegetable oil
1 onion, chopped
1 garlic clove, crushed
198 g (7 oz) can chopped tomatoes
1 tbls Worcestershire sauce
1 tsp brown sugar
few drops Tabasco sauce
salt and pepper

Heat the margarine in a medium saucepan. Add the onion and cook for 2 minutes or until tender.

Stir in the rice and cook for 3 minutes. Add the stock, salt and pepper and bring to the boil, then reduce the heat and cover.

Cook gently for 10 minutes or until all the liquid has been absorbed and the grains are soft.

Leave the rice mixture until very cold. Using wetted hands, place a spoonful of rice in one hand.

Place a mushroom with a cube of cheese in the centre of the rice and form it into a neat ball, completely covering the mushroom and cheese. Press to make a firm ball.

Place on a plate and make another 19 balls. Coat each rice ball evenly in beaten egg and breadcrumbs, then chill until required.

To make the sauce: heat the oil in a small saucepan, add the onion and garlic and cook gently for 2 minutes.

Stir in the tomatoes, Worcestershire sauce, sugar, Tabasco sauce, salt and pepper.

Bring to the boil, then reduce the heat and cook for 2 minutes. Pour into a warmed dish to serve.

Heat the oil in a deep fat fryer to 190°C (375°F) or until a cube of stale bread browns in 30 seconds.

Add half the rice croquettes and fry for 4-5 minutes, or until crisp and golden brown.

Drain on absorbent paper and keep warm while frying the remaining croquettes.

Serve on a warmed serving dish garnished with sprigs of parsley and lemon wedges and serve with the spicy sauce.

Chilli rice courgettes

SERVES 4

4 large courgettes
1 tbls vegetable oil
1 small onion, chopped
50 g (2 oz) button mushrooms,
*   chopped*
1 tsp chopped red chilli or ½ tsp
*   chilli powder*
2 tomatoes, skinned, seeded and
*   chopped*
1 tbls tomato purée
2 tbls cottage cheese
salt and pepper
75 g (3 oz) brown rice
200 ml (⅓ pint) chicken or
*   vegetable stock*
1 tbls grated Parmesan cheese
To garnish:
chilli slices and chervil sprigs

Heat the oven to 190°C, 375°F, Gas Mark 5. Top and tail the courgettes, cut in half lengthways and scoop out the flesh, leaving the shells whole. Chop the flesh finely.

Heat the oil in a medium saucepan, add the courgette flesh, onion, mushrooms and chilli. Cook for 2-3 minutes, stirring occasionally.

Add the tomatoes, tomato purée, cottage cheese, some salt and pepper and the rice. Cook for 2 minutes.

Stir in the stock, bring to the boil and reduce the heat. Cover the pan and simmer for 10-15 minutes until the liquid is absorbed.

Place the courgette shells in a frying pan of boiling water and cook for 3 minutes, then drain well and place in a shallow ovenproof dish.

Fill each courgette with the rice mixture and sprinkle with Parmesan cheese. Cook for 20-25 minutes until courgettes are tender. Garnish with chilli slices and chervil sprigs.

• **Chilli rice courgettes; Rice croquettes with spicy sauce**

Luxury rice pudding

SERVES 4

15 g (½ oz) butter
50 g (2 oz) short-grain rice
600 ml (1 pint) milk
284 ml (10 fl oz) carton single
* cream*
15 g (½ oz) caster sugar
10 g (½ oz) butter
¼ tsp grated nutmeg

Heat the oven to 160°C, 325°F, Gas
Mark 3. Butter a 1.2 litre (2 pint)
shallow ovenproof dish.

Place the rice, milk, cream, sugar,
butter and nutmeg into the dish and
stir until well blended.

Cook in the centre of the oven for
1¾-2 hours (stir once, halfway
through cooking) until the pudding
is thick and creamy and golden
brown on top.

Serving idea: Serve hot with stewed
plums or apple, or cold with sliced
fresh fruit and cream. Or flavour the
rice with orange or lemon rind, or
1 tbls marmalade.

Eastern delight

SERVES 4

50 g (2 oz) ground rice
600 ml (1 pint) milk
1 tbls caster sugar
2 tsp rose water (optional)
½ tsp ground cinnamon
142 ml (5 fl oz) carton double
* cream, whipped*
10 g (½ oz) pistachio nuts, skinned
* and chopped or flaked almonds,*
* toasted*
4 figs, fresh or dried, sliced

Place the ground rice in a medium
saucepan and stir in the milk
gradually until well blended.

Bring to the boil, stirring continuously, until the mixture thick-
ens. Reduce the heat and cook
gently for 3-4 minutes.

Stir in the caster sugar, rose
water and cinnamon, then cover the
surface with cling film and chill.

Add the cream to the rice mixture
and fold in carefully until evenly
mixed. Divide half of the mixture
between 4 individual glasses. Reserve 4 slices of fig for decoration
and arrange the remainder in the
glasses. Top with remaining rice
mixture, and decorate with sliced
figs and pistachio nuts.

● Luxury rice pudding; Eastern delight;
Rice fritters with raspberry sauce

Rice fritters with raspberry sauce

MAKES 16

600 ml (1 pint) milk
50 g (2 oz) short-grain rice
1 tsp vanilla essence
1 tbls caster sugar
1 egg, beaten
50 g (2 oz) fresh white breadcrumbs
oil for frying
whole raspberries, to decorate
For the sauce:
225 g (8 oz) raspberries, thawed if
*   frozen*
3 tbls icing sugar

Place the milk in a medium saucepan and bring to the boil. Stir in the rice and vanilla essence and reduce the heat.

Simmer for 20 minutes until the milk is absorbed and the rice soft. Stir in 1 tbls of sugar. Spread the mixture into a square 18 cm (7 inch) tin. Leave until cold.

Cut the rice mixture into 16 squares and dip each square into egg and breadcrumbs.

For the sauce: place the raspberries in a liquidizer goblet with 2 tbls icing sugar. Run the machine until the sauce is well blended.

Sieve to remove the pips and place in a serving jug.

Heat about 2.5 cm (1 inch) of oil in a small frying pan and when hot carefully fry 3 fritters for 2-3 minutes until golden brown.

Turn once and fry the second side. Drain on absorbent paper.

Place on a warmed serving plate and sprinkle with remaining icing sugar and decorate with whole raspberries. Serve with raspberry sauce.

Orange rice shortbread

MAKES 12 WEDGES

100 g (4 oz) plain flour
50 g (2 oz) ground rice
25 g (1 oz) caster sugar
100 g (4 oz) unsalted butter,
*   softened*
rind of 1 orange, grated

Heat the oven to 160°C, 325°F, Gas Mark 3. Place the flour, ground rice and sugar in a bowl.

Add the butter and grated orange rind and rub in finely with the fingers until the mixture begins to bind together.

Knead into a soft dough and place on a lightly floured surface. Roll out to a 20 cm (8 inch) round.

Place on a lightly floured baking sheet, score around the edge with a fork and mark into 12 wedges with a knife. Prick all over with a fork.

Cook in the centre of the oven for 35-40 minutes or until lightly browned at the edges.

Cool on a wire rack and cut into wedges while still warm.

The shortbread may be stored in a container for several weeks.

Bruléed rice custard

MAKES 6 INDIVIDUAL CUSTARDS

300 ml (½ pint) milk
3 eggs
1 tbls caster sugar
rind of 1 orange, grated
425 g (15 oz) can creamed rice
*   pudding*
6 tsp soft light brown sugar
1 orange, segmented, to garnish

Heat the oven to 160°C, 325°F, Gas Mark 3. Place the milk in a saucepan and bring to the boil.

Whisk the eggs and sugar together in a bowl and slowly whisk in the milk. Add grated orange rind and mix together with the rice pudding, then strain the egg mixture into the rice and stir well together.

Ladle the rice custard into 6 individual ramekin dishes and place the dishes in a roasting tin.

Half-fill the tin with hot water, then place just above the centre of the oven for 45 minutes to 1 hour until custard has set.

Test by piercing the custard with the blade of a knife; if cooked, the blade should come out cleanly.

Remove the dishes from the roasting tin and leave until quite cold.

Peel the white pith from the orange and cut out the segments with a sharp knife.

Just before serving, sprinkle the top of each custard with brown sugar and place under a hot grill for 2-3 minutes until caramelized.

Leave to cool for a few minutes, then decorate each with a few orange segments. Or serve the rice custard warm without sugar topping, or as the recipe with some pouring cream.

● Orange rice shortbread; Bruléed rice custard; Summer rice cheescake

Summer rice cheesecake

SERVES 8

For the base:
75 g (3 oz) unsalted butter
200 g (7 oz) packet digestive
 biscuits, crushed
For the filling:
100 g (4 oz) unsalted butter
150 g (5 oz) lemon
 flavour jelly
227 g (8 oz) low-fat soft or skimmed
 milk cheese
425 g (15 oz) can creamed rice
 pudding
grated rind and juice of 1 lemon
For the topping:
1 kiwi fruit, sliced
8 strawberries, hulled and sliced
1 tbls redcurrant jelly or sieved
 jam, melted
whole strawberries and leaves to
 decorate

Melt the butter in a small saucepan and stir in the biscuits.

Press the mixture over the base of a 20 cm (8 inch) loose-based cake tin using a metal spoon.

To make the filling: place the butter and jelly in a saucepan and heat gently, stirring occasionally, until melted.

Pour into a liquidizer goblet with the cheese and blend well.

Add the rice, grated lemon rind and juice and stir until well mixed.

Pour over the biscuit base in the tin and leave for about 1½ hours in a cool place to set.

Carefully remove the cheesecake from tin, slide off the base and place on a serving plate.

Decorate the top of the cheesecake with halved slices of kiwi fruit and strawberry slices. Brush fruit with redcurrant jelly or jam to glaze. Place leaves and whole strawberries around the base of cheesecake.

The Italians discovered long ago the many wonderful recipes that can be created with pasta. There are numerous shapes and sizes available and a whole range of exciting sauces to serve with them.

Traditional pasta is made from the best quality Durum wheat which has been milled into a fine flour then mixed with water and kneaded into a smooth dough. This was originally done by hand but is now, of course, done by machine.

It is the kneading and stretching that is the vital part of making pasta. Once the dough is ready, it can be rolled out or passed through a pasta machine where it is made into all the different shapes that you see on sale.

This plain pasta dough can be flavoured and coloured by adding egg, spinach (to make Pasta Verde) or even tomato. However, there is now another type available – wholewheat. This is not a traditional pasta but one that has been developed in recent years. It is made from a different type of wheat flour that is not refined as much and is softer. Wholewheat pasta is brown, has a good flavour and a little more fibre than other pasta.

Most pasta sold in this country is dried but there are some fresh varieties available and a few people have taken to making their own at home.

The way pasta is cooked is very important but quite simple. The key is to use a large amount of lightly salted boiling water and cook the pasta quickly until it is 'al dente' – tender without being soft or sticky. Cooking time varies according to the shape and size and it is best to follow the instructions on the pack. Most dried varieties will cook in about 10 minutes, fresh or home-made take a little less time. Make sure the water is kept at a constant rolling boil and stir occasionally with a wooden fork or spoon. When it is cooked, drain the pasta, season with black pepper and serve immediately.

Here are some brief descriptions of the types of pasta available.

1

4

2

3

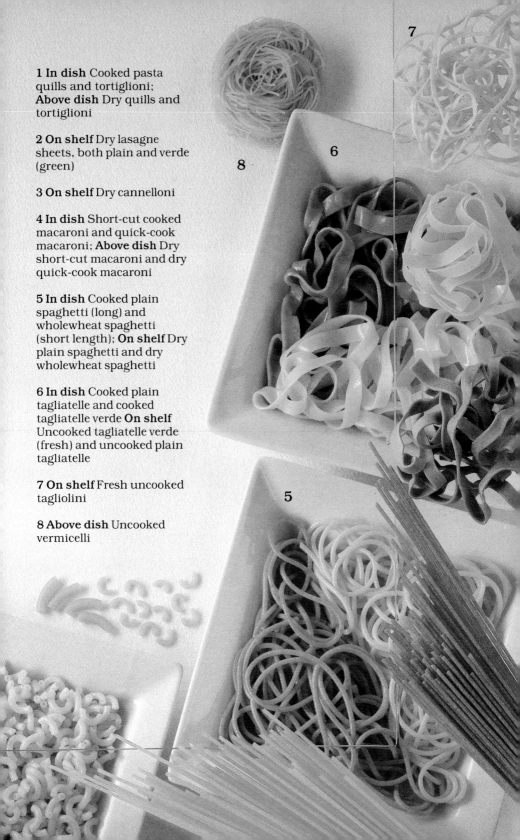

1 In dish Cooked pasta quills and tortiglioni; **Above dish** Dry quills and tortiglioni

2 On shelf Dry lasagne sheets, both plain and verde (green)

3 On shelf Dry cannelloni

4 In dish Short-cut cooked macaroni and quick-cook macaroni; **Above dish** Dry short-cut macaroni and dry quick-cook macaroni

5 In dish Cooked plain spaghetti (long) and wholewheat spaghetti (short length); **On shelf** Dry plain spaghetti and dry wholewheat spaghetti

6 In dish Cooked plain tagliatelle and cooked tagliatelle verde **On shelf** Uncooked tagliatelle verde (fresh) and uncooked plain tagliatelle

7 On shelf Fresh uncooked tagliolini

8 Above dish Uncooked vermicelli

Cannelloni (Large tubes)
These fat tubes of pasta are filled with a savoury meat or chicken filling then baked in a sauce.

Conchiglie (Shells)
Shell-shaped pasta shapes served with a sauce or as an accompaniment or cold in salads.

Farfalle (Bows)
Pretty bows and butterfly shapes can be added to soups and stews, served as an accompaniment or cold in salads.

Lasagne (Ribbons)
These are a type of wide ribbon pasta, either plain, wholewheat or with added spinach.

Lumachine (Snails)
Little snail-shaped shapes used for garnishing soups.

Macaroni (Small tubes)
This tube-like pasta can be either long-stranded, short-cut or curved (elbow *macaroni*).

Manicotti (Ribbed tubes)
Similar to *cannelloni*, *manicotti* (little muffs) are wide ribbed tubes.

Pappardelle (Ribbons)
A very broad pasta or ribbon noodle usually cut to give a fluted edge.

Penne (Quills)
Small tubes – similar to cannelloni – with quill shaped ends.

Ravioli (Filled squares)
This classic pasta savoury is made from little squares pressed together round a savoury filling.

Rigatoni (Ribbed tubes)
A wide, ribbed *macaroni* usually baked in a meat and tomato sauce.

Ruote (Wheels)
Wheel-shaped pasta which are good baked or pre-cooked and stir-fried with meat or vegetables.

Semini (Rice shapes)
These look like grains of rice and are used for garnishing soups.

Spaghetti (Strands)
Familiar as long, solid strands of pasta, *spaghetti* can be obtained in several widths and can be either plain or wholewheat, spinach-flavoured or quick-cook.

Tagliatelle (Ribbon noodles)
These ribbon noodles are sold either fresh or dried, with or without eggs and spinach added.

Tortellini (Filled triangles)
These are formed from small circles of pasta dough folded in half over a filling of either meat or ricotta cheese and parsley.

Tortiglioni (Twist)
These are the popular twists and corkscrew shapes served as an accompaniment or topped with a sauce.

Vermicelli (Thin strands)
Long, fine strands of *spaghetti*-like pasta which are usually broken into shorter lengths and used in soups.

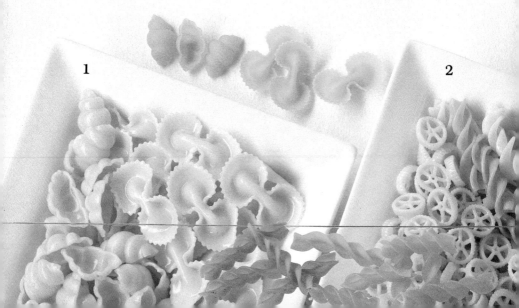

1

2

1 In dish Cooked pasta
shells and cooked pasta
bows; **Above dish** Dry
pasta shells and dry pasta
bows; **On shelf** Dry verde
twists and dry orange
twists

2 In dish Cooked pasta
wheels and cooked multi-
coloured twists; **On shelf**
Dry pasta wheels

3 Dry animal pasta shapes

4 In dish Cooked tortellini
and cooked ravioli;
On shelf Dry ravioli,
fresh large ravioli and
dry tortellini

5 In dish Cooked fresh
capelletti and cooked
fresh tortelloni; **On shelf**
Fresh tortelloni and fresh
capelletti, uncooked

6 Beside dish Pasta shells

BASIC PASTA SAUCES

Bolognese sauce

This is always a handy sauce to make in quantity and freeze. An ideal partner for spaghetti and rice as well as a base for lasagne or a quick Moussaka.

SERVES 4

1 tbls vegetable oil
50 g (2 oz) bacon, rinded and
  chopped or Prosciutto, chopped
1 onion, finely chopped
1 garlic clove, crushed
2 sticks celery, finely chopped
1 carrot, finely chopped
100 g (4 oz) button mushrooms,
  finely chopped
225 g (8 oz) minced beef
4 large ripe tomatoes, skinned,
  seeded and chopped
2 tbls tomato purée
150 ml (¼ pint) red wine
150 ml (¼ pint) beef or vegetable
  stock
1 tsp caster sugar
salt and pepper
1 bay leaf

Heat the oil in a medium saucepan, add the bacon or Prosciutto, onion, garlic, celery, carrot and mushrooms.

Cook rapidly for 2 minutes, stirring occasionally. Stir in the beef and cook until brown. Add the tomatoes, tomato purée, wine, stock, sugar, some salt and pepper and the bay leaf.

Bring to the boil, reduce the heat and cover the saucepan with a lid. Cook gently for 45-50 minutes, giving an occasional stir.

Serving idea: Serve with any variety of pasta and either fresh or pre-grated Parmesan cheese.

Fresh tomato sauce

There is nothing quite like the real taste of fresh tomato sauce with a hint of fresh basil. Make it in large quantities when tomatoes are in season and freeze it in small portions.

SERVES 4-6

1 tbls olive oil
1 stick celery, chopped
1 carrot, chopped
2 onions, chopped
2 garlic cloves, crushed
1 kg (2¼ lb) ripe large tomatoes,
  quartered
2 tsp caster sugar
salt and pepper
2 tbls chopped fresh basil

Heat the oil in a medium saucepan, add the celery, carrot, onion and garlic. Cook gently for 3 minutes until tender.

Stir in the tomatoes, sugar, salt and pepper and the basil. Bring to the boil, reduce the heat and cover the saucepan with a lid.

Cook gently for 30 minutes, then place in a liquidizer goblet and run the machine until the sauce is well blended.

Serving idea: Serve sauce hot with cooked spaghetti, tagliatelle or pasta shapes. Also serve with Pasta pillows (p. 54) as a pouring or dipping sauce.

● From top: Fresh tomato sauce with pasta bows; Dry ravioli; Quick tomato sauce with green pasta twists; Dry tortellini; Bolognese sauce with wholemeal spaghetti; Plain dry spaghetti.

Quick tomato sauce

SERVES 4-6

1 tbls olive oil
2 onions, finely chopped
2 garlic cloves, crushed
2 × 397 g (14 oz) cans chopped
  tomatoes
2 tsp caster sugar
½ tsp Worcestershire sauce,
  optional
salt and pepper
2 tbls chopped fresh or 1 tbls dried
  basil

Heat the oil in a medium saucepan. Add the onions and garlic and cook gently for 5-6 minutes or until tender.

Stir in the tomatoes, sugar, Worcestershire sauce, if using, salt and pepper and the basil. Bring to the boil and cook rapidly for about 5 minutes, or until the sauce has thickened.

Serving idea: Serve tomato sauce with all varieties of pasta, sprinkled with Parmesan cheese and garnished with fresh basil.

Sauce alla Amatriciana

Originating from the Abruzzi region of Italy, this traditional, country sauce makes a tasty accompaniment to most types of pasta. It is particularly suited to the tubular variety such as rigatoni or macaroni.

SERVES 4

1 tbls sunflower or olive oil
75 g (3 oz) lean, unsmoked bacon, rinded and diced
1 small onion, finely chopped
1 canned pimiento, chopped
350 g (12 oz) fresh tomatoes, skinned and chopped (see note)
salt and pepper

Heat the oil in a heavy pan, add the bacon and fry gently for 5 minutes until golden. Remove with a slotted spoon, put on one side and keep hot.

In the same pan, fry the onion until transparent, then add the pimiento, tomatoes, bacon and seasoning to taste.

Cook briskly for 10 minutes, stirring all the time.

Note: To skin tomatoes, place in boiling water for 1-2 minutes. The skins can then be removed easily.

Serving idea: When the pasta is cooked, pile into a serving dish and spoon the sauce on top. Sprinkle with grated Parmesan or Pecorino cheese (which is available in Italian supermarkets or delicatessens). Garnish with a sprig of fresh coriander leaves and serve immediately.

Variation: Add 2 tbls of wine or vermouth with the tomatoes. Add some fresh chopped red chilli with the pimiento for a slightly stronger flavour.

Italian vegetable sauce

A useful sauce to make when summer vegetables are plentiful. Take advantage of seasonal availability and make in bulk for the freezer. This very versatile sauce is good just with plain boiled pasta, but also for layering pasta before baking, or replacing tomato sauce.

SERVES 4

1 tbls oil
1 onion, finely chopped
1 red pepper, seeded and finely
    chopped
1 yellow pepper, seeded and finely
    chopped
2 sticks celery, finely chopped
1 courgette, finely chopped
4 tomatoes, skinned, seeded and
    chopped
225 g (8 oz) spinach leaves,
    chopped
150 ml (¼ pint) vegetable stock or
    water
salt and pepper
1 tsp caster sugar

Heat the oil in a large saucepan, add the onion, peppers, celery and courgette and cook for 2 minutes until almost tender.

Stir in the tomatoes, spinach, stock, some salt and pepper and the sugar. Bring to the boil and cook for 10 minutes until the sauce has reduced and is thick.

Serving idea: Serve with fresh or dried cooked pasta or use in lasagne for a different filling. It also makes a good filling for a quiche with beaten eggs added.

• Italian vegetable sauce with pasta quills; Dry lasagne sheets; Pesto sauce with tagliatelle; Dry cannelloni; Seafood sauce on pasta shells; Dry wholemeal spaghetti

Seafood sauce

The delicate flavour of fish and the creamy texture make this sauce rather special to serve with pasta. Try replacing the mussels and scallops with crab or lobster for a change in flavour, or serve it liquidized to make a creamy soup.

SERVES 4

50 g (2 oz) butter or margarine
1 onion, finely chopped
1 garlic clove, crushed
50 g (2 oz) plain flour
450 ml (¾ pint) vegetable stock
150 ml (¼ pint) white wine
100 g (4 oz) halibut, cubed
6 scallops, cut into quarters
50 g (2 oz) canned or frozen
    mussels
100 g (4 oz) peeled prawns
1 tbls chopped fresh marjoram
salt and pepper
142 ml (5 fl oz) carton single cream

Melt the butter in a medium saucepan, add the onion and garlic, and cook gently for 2 minutes.

Stir in the flour and cook for 1 minute. Gradually add the stock and the wine, stirring continuously, and bring to the boil.

Reduce the heat and stir in the halibut and scallops and cook gently for 2-3 minutes.

Stir in the mussels, prawns and marjoram and some salt and pepper and heat gently for 1 minute.

Just before serving, add the cream and heat through.

Serving idea: Serve with tagliatelle verde or plain garnished with a lemon cone and sprig of rosemary as a starter, or as a main meal. Mix cooked pasta shapes into the sauce, sprinkle with cheese and grill for a quick supper dish.

Variation: Liquidize the sauce before adding cream, then gently reheat. Add the cream, but do not bring to the boil.

45

Buttered tagliatelle with parmesan

SERVES 4

1 ½ litres (3 pints) water
1 tsp salt
1 tbls oil
225g (8oz) tagliatelle plain
   or verde
40 g (1 ½ oz) butter
black pepper
2 tbls grated Parmesan cheese
1 tbls chopped fresh parsley

Place the water, salt and oil in a large saucepan and bring to the boil.

Add the tagliatelle, keeping the water boiling.

Reduce the heat slightly and cook for 8-10 minutes, stirring occasionally, until tender.

Drain the tagliatelle, rinse with hot water and drain in a sieve.

Place the butter in the saucepan and melt. Add the tagliatelle and toss to coat evenly with butter.

Transfer the pasta to a warmed serving dish or individual dishes and sprinkle with some pepper, Parmesan cheese and parsley.

Serving idea: Serve as a starter as it is, or accompanied by one of the sauces, followed by a main meal of grilled fish or meat with salad.

Crispy fried noodles

SERVES 4

1 ½ litres (3 pints) water
1 tsp salt
1 tbls vegetable oil
175 g (6 oz) tagliatelle
oil for deep frying

Place the water, salt and oil in a large saucepan and bring to the boil.

Add the tagliatelle to the saucepan, keeping the water boiling.

Reduce the heat slightly and cook the tagliatelle for 8-10 minutes, stirring occasionally, until tender.

Drain the tagliatelle, rinse with hot water and drain thoroughly in a sieve. Then form into 12 small nests using a spoon and fork. Place on a plate until cold.

Heat the oil in a deep fat fryer to 190°C, 375°F or until a cube of stale bread browns in 30 seconds.

Fry 2 or 3 nests at a time for about 3 minutes until crisp and brown.

Drain on absorbent paper and keep warm while frying the remaining nests. Serve hot.

Serving idea: Serve as an accompaniment to soup, or as a contrast in texture with soufflés, mornays and au gratins. Or fry onion rings tossed in flour and serve with loose tagliatelle deep fried.

Spaghetti with herbed garlic oil

SERVES 4

1 ½ litres (3 pints) water
1 tsp salt
1 tbls vegetable oil
225 g (8 oz) plain or wholewheat
   spaghetti
4 lemon wedges, to garnish
For the dressing:
3 tbls olive oil
2 garlic cloves, crushed
1 tbls chopped fresh basil
1 tbls chopped fresh marjoram
1 tbls chopped fresh coriander
black pepper

Place the water, salt and oil in a large saucepan and bring to the boil.

Coil the spaghetti into the saucepan, keeping the water boiling.

Reduce the heat slightly and cook for 8-10 minutes, stirring occasionally, until the spaghetti is tender.

Drain the spaghetti, rinse with hot water and drain thoroughly.

Place the dressing ingredients in the saucepan. Add the spaghetti and toss well to coat evenly.

Place in a warmed serving dish or serve individually with a wedge of lemon.

Serving idea: Serve spaghetti with a tomato and Mozzarella salad or a mixed green salad.

Variation: Try a different mixture of herbs in season.

● From top: Spaghetti with herbed garlic oil; Crispy fried noodles; Buttered tagliatelle with parmesan

Chicken vermicelli soup

SERVES 4

½ tbls vegetable oil
2 chicken quarters, skinned
1 onion, chopped
1 carrot, chopped
1 stick celery, chopped
1¼ litres (2½ pints) chicken stock
salt and pepper
40 g (1½ oz) vermicelli, roughly
   broken
1 tbls chopped fresh parsley, to
   garnish

Heat the oil in a large saucepan. Add the chicken joints and lightly brown.

Stir in the onion, carrot and celery and cook gently for 5 minutes.

Add the stock and some salt and pepper and bring to the boil. Reduce the heat and cover the saucepan with a lid. Cook gently for 1 hour. Remove the chicken from the soup and cut the meat off the bones.

Strain the soup, return it to the saucepan and bring to the boil.

Add the vermicelli, keeping the soup boiling, then reduce the heat slightly and cook for 5 minutes.

Stir in the chicken pieces and pour the soup into a warmed tureen or individual bowls. Sprinkle with chopped parsley.

Mixed vegetable and pasta soup

SERVES 4

25 g (1 oz) butter
1 onion, chopped
1 small leek, trimmed and sliced
1 carrot, diced
1 small turnip, diced
1 stick celery, sliced
¼ small green cabbage, shredded
1¼ litres (2½ pints) vegetable stock
   or water
salt and pepper
50 g (2 oz) quick-cook macaroni
1 tbls chopped fresh parsley
grated Parmesan cheese

Melt the butter in a large saucepan. Add the onion, leek, carrot, turnip and celery.

Cook gently for 5 minutes, stirring occasionally. Stir in the cabbage, stock and some salt and pepper and bring to the boil.

Add the macaroni, keeping the soup boiling, and stir well.

Reduce the heat slightly and cook for 15 minutes until the macaroni is tender.

Serve the soup in a warmed tureen or individual bowls, sprinkle with parsley, and offer a separate bowl of Parmesan cheese.

Serving idea: Serve as a main meal soup with French bread and butter and a selection of cheeses.

Variation: This soup can be made with any seasonal vegetables.

• Mixed vegetable and pasta soup; Chicken vermicelli soup; Seafood pasta mornay

Seafood pasta mornay

SERVES 4

900 ml (1½ pints) water
1 tsp salt
1 tbls vegetable oil
50 g (2 oz) pasta bows
For the sauce and filling:
50 g (2 oz) butter or margarine
50 g (2 oz) plain flour
450 ml (¾ pint) milk
¼ tsp mustard
salt and pepper
75 g (3 oz) Cheddar cheese, grated
3 tbls grated Parmesan cheese
175 g (6 oz) smoked mackerel fillet,
*   skinned and chopped*
100 g (4 oz) peeled prawns
1 tbls chopped fresh parsley
To garnish:
sprigs of parsley
8 cooked pasta bows
4 prawns

Place water, salt and oil in a medium saucepan and bring to the boil. Add the pasta bows to the saucepan, keeping the water boiling. Reduce the heat slightly and cook for 8-10 minutes, stirring occasionally, until the pasta is tender.

Drain the pasta, rinse with hot water and drain thoroughly.

To make the sauce: melt the butter in a saucepan, add the flour and cook for 1 minute. Gradually add the milk, off the heat.

Bring to the boil, stirring, over a moderate heat for 2 minutes, add the mustard, salt and pepper.

Reserve one-third of each cheese and add the remainder to the sauce with the pasta, mackerel, prawns and parsley. Stir, then divide between 4 flameproof dishes or scallop shells. Sprinkle the remaining cheese over the top of each dish.

Just before serving, place the dishes in a grill pan under a moderate grill. Cook for 8-10 minutes until hot and lightly browned. Serve garnished with parsley sprigs, pasta bows and prawns.

Cheese pasta soufflés

SERVES 6

900 ml (1 ½ pints) water
1 tsp salt
1 tbls vegetable oil
50 g (2 oz) small pasta shells
For the sauce:
50 g (2 oz) butter or margarine
50 g (2 oz) plain flour
300 ml (½ pint) milk
¼ tsp mustard
salt and pepper
75 g (3 oz) mature Cheddar cheese,
  grated
4 tbls grated Parmesan cheese
3 egg yolks
4 egg whites

Place water, salt and oil in a medium saucepan and bring to the boil.

Add pasta shells to the saucepan, keeping the water boiling.

Reduce the heat slightly and cook for 8-10 minutes, stirring occasionally, until the pasta is tender.

Drain the pasta, rinse with hot water and drain thoroughly in a sieve. Heat the oven to 180°C, 350°F, Gas Mark 4.

To make the sauce: melt the butter in a saucepan, add the flour and cook for 1 minute. Gradually add the milk, off the heat, beating all the time.

Bring to the boil, stirring, over a moderate heat and cook for 1 minute.

Stir in the mustard, salt and pepper, Cheddar cheese, 2 tbls of Parmesan and the egg yolks and beat well together.

Whisk the egg whites until stiff, add to the sauce with the pasta shells and fold in carefully until evenly mixed.

Divide the mixture between 6 individual soufflé dishes or place in one large dish, each buttered and sprinkled with a little Parmesan cheese.

Cook in the centre of the oven for 25-30 minutes for the small soufflés or 40-45 minutes for the large soufflé.

Serve immediately.

Serving idea: Serve as a starter or a main dish with a selection of vegetables in season, or with a mixed salad and crusty bread.

Variation: Replace half of the cheese with chopped ham or mushrooms and try wholewheat pasta.

Pasta twists with walnut sauce

SERVES 4

1 ½ litres (3 pints) water
1 tsp salt
1 tbls vegetable oil
225 g (8 oz) pasta twists
butter
340 g (12 oz) can asparagus,
  drained and sliced
For the sauce:
65 ml (4 tbls) olive or walnut oil
2 garlic cloves, crushed
4 tbls chopped fresh parsley
75 g (3 oz) walnuts, finely ground
50 g (2 oz) pine nuts or cashew
  nuts, finely ground
150 ml (¼ pint) hot water
1 egg, beaten
2 tbls single cream
To garnish:
asparagus spears
walnut halves

Place the water, salt and oil in a large saucepan and bring to the boil.

Add the pasta to the saucepan, keeping the water boiling.

Reduce the heat slightly and cook for 8-10 minutes, stirring occasionally, until pasta is tender.

Drain pasta, rinse with hot water and drain thoroughly in a sieve.

Melt a little butter in the saucepan and toss pasta to coat evenly. Add the asparagus and stir the mixture well.

To make the sauce: heat the oil in

a frying pan, add the garlic and parsley and fry for 1 minute.

Add the nuts and fry gently until golden brown, stirring occasionally, then remove the frying pan from the heat.

Stir together the hot water, egg and cream until well blended. Then add to the nut mixture and stir well until completely blended.

Spoon over the pasta and toss well. Place the mixture on a warmed serving plate and garnish with asparagus spears and walnut halves.

The sauce may be kept for up to 3 days in a refrigerator. Reheat gently, but do not boil.

● Cheese pasta soufflés; Pasta twists with walnut sauce

Spaghetti alla Genovese

This delicious sauce can be eaten with all kinds of pasta and is also good stirred into minestrone soup. It will keep for up to 2 weeks in a screwtop jar in the refrigerator.

SERVES 4

1½ litres (3 pints) water
1 tsp salt
1 tbls vegetable oil
225 g (8 oz) spaghetti
For the sauce:
3 garlic cloves
¼ tsp salt
40 g (1½ oz) walnuts
25 g (1 oz) fresh basil leaves, finely chopped
50 g (2 oz) grated Parmesan cheese
150 ml (¼ pint) olive oil
fresh basil leaves

Place all the ingredients for the sauce in an electric blender and blend until smooth.

Alternatively use a mortar and pestle to pound the garlic and salt together then add the walnuts and then the basil a little at a time, pounding until the mixture is like a purée. Mix in alternate spoonfuls of cheese and oil.

Place the water, salt and oil in a large saucepan and bring to the boil.

Coil the pasta into the saucepan, keeping the water boiling.

Reduce the heat slightly and cook for 8-10 minutes, stirring occasionally until the pasta is tender or *al dente*.

Drain the pasta, and pile onto a warmed serving dish, mix in half the sauce, and hand the rest separately. Garnish with fresh basil leaves.

Florentine pasta quiche

SERVES 4-6

175 g (6 oz) wholemeal flour
75 g (3 oz) margarine
1½ tbls cold water to mix
For the filling:
900 ml (1½ pints) water
1 tsp salt
1 tbls vegetable oil
75 g (3 oz) pasta wheels
100 g (4 oz) cooked, chopped spinach
113 g (4 oz) carton cottage cheese
2 tbls grated Parmesan cheese
3 eggs, beaten
142 ml (5 fl oz) carton single cream
150 ml (¼ pint) milk
¼ tsp grated nutmeg
salt and pepper
tomatoes and chervil, to garnish

Place the flour in a bowl, add the margarine and rub in finely with the fingers until the mixture resembles breadcrumbs.

Stir in the water and mix with a fork to form a firm dough. Knead lightly on a floured surface.

Roll out the pastry and line a 23 cm (9 inch) loose-based flan tin. Prick the base and chill the pastry case.

Heat the oven to 200°C, 400°F, Gas Mark 6. Line the pastry case with greaseproof paper, fill with baking beans and cook in the oven for 10-15 minutes to set the pastry. Remove beans and paper.

To make the filling: place the water, salt and oil in a medium saucepan. Add the pasta to the saucepan, keeping the water boiling.

Reduce the heat slightly and cook

● Florentine pasta quiche; Spaghetti alla Genovese

the pasta for 8-10 minutes, stirring occasionally. Drain the pasta, rinse with hot water and drain thoroughly in a sieve, then place in a bowl.

Add the spinach, cottage and Parmesan cheeses, eggs, cream, milk, nutmeg and some salt and pepper.

Stir well and pour the mixture into the pastry case.

Reduce the oven to 160°C, 325°F,

Gas Mark 3 and cook for 30-40 minutes until the filling has set.

Leave to cool in the tin before placing on a serving plate. Serve warm or cold, garnished with sliced tomatoes and chervil.

Serving idea: Serve with new potatoes and a mixed salad, pitta bread and butter.

Pasta pillows

SERVES 4

900 ml (1 ½ pints) water
1 tsp salt
1 tbls vegetable oil
8 cannelloni tubes
butter
For the filling:
225 g (8 oz) low-fat soft cheese
1 egg, beaten
1 tbls grated Parmesan cheese
50 g (2 oz) fresh white breadcrumbs
1 tbls chopped fresh parsley
1 garlic clove, crushed
6 streaky bacon rashers, grilled
  and chopped
salt and pepper
For the batter:
100 g (4 oz) self-raising flour
salt
1 tbls vegetable oil
1 egg, beaten
150 ml (¼ pint) water
oil for deep frying
To garnish:
lemon slices
parsley sprigs

Place water, salt and oil in a medium saucepan and bring to the boil.

Add the cannelloni to the saucepan, keeping the water boiling. Reduce the heat and cook for 6-8 minutes, stirring occasionally, until the pasta is tender.

Drain the pasta, rinse with hot water and drain thoroughly in a sieve, then place on a plate to cool.

To make the filling: place the cheese, egg, Parmesan, breadcrumbs, parsley and garlic in a bowl. Beat together with a wooden spoon until well blended. Stir in the bacon and some salt and pepper.

Cut the cannelloni tubes in half widthways to make 16 tubes and fill each with some filling. Press ends together lightly.

To make the batter: place the flour, some salt, the oil and egg in a mixing bowl.

Stir in half the water and mix together with a wooden spoon until smooth, then beat well.

Beat in the remaining water to make a coating batter.

Heat the oil in a deep fat fryer to 190°C, 375°F or until a cube of stale bread browns in 30 seconds.

Dip 4 pasta pillows in batter and place them in the hot oil. Fry for 3-4 minutes until golden brown.

Drain on absorbent paper and place on a warmed serving dish. Keep warm while frying the remaining pasta pillows.

Serve garnished with lemon slices and parsley sprigs.

Serving idea: Serve hot with Pesto or Tomato sauce, pitta bread and green salad.

Note: Pasta pillows may be frozen. Thaw to room temperature before coating in batter and deep frying.

• Pasta pillows; Chinese chilli noodles

Chinese chilli noodles

SERVES 4

1½ litres (3 pints) water
1 tsp salt
1 tbls vegetable oil
225 g (8 oz) Chinese noodles or
   vermicelli
butter
3 tbls sunflower or sesame seed oil
1 garlic clove, crushed
1 tsp chopped fresh green chilli
225 g (8 oz) pork tenderloin, finely
   sliced
4 sticks frozen crab meat, thawed
   and sliced
100 g (4 oz) peeled prawns
350 g (12 oz) bamboo shoots, cut
   into strips
1 tbls hot chilli sauce
To garnish:
slices of red and green chilli
strips of bamboo shoots

Place the water, salt and vegetable oil in a large saucepan and bring to the boil before adding pasta.

Add the noodles or vermicelli to the saucepan, keeping the water boiling. Reduce the heat slightly and cook for 3 minutes, stirring occasionally, until firm but not tender.

Drain the noodles or vermicelli, rinse with hot water and drain thoroughly in a sieve.

Melt a little butter in the saucepan and toss the pasta to coat evenly.

Heat 1 tbls sunflower oil in a large frying pan, add the garlic, chilli and pork and fry quickly for 1 minute.

Stir in the crab, prawns, bamboo shoots and chilli sauce and cook for 1 minute, then pour into a bowl.

Heat the remaining oil in the frying pan and add the vermicelli.

Fry quickly, stirring occasionally, until the vermicelli is lightly browned.

Add the ingredients in the bowl to the vermicelli and stir carefully until well mixed.

Arrange the chilli noodles in a warmed serving dish and garnish.

Three-cheese macaroni

SERVES 4

1½ litres (3 pints) water
1 tsp salt
1 tbls vegetable oil
225 g (8 oz) wholewheat macaroni
butter
For the sauce:
50 g (2 oz) butter or margarine
50 g (2 oz) plain flour
½ tsp mustard
cayenne pepper
¼ tsp salt
1 tsp Worcestershire sauce
725 ml (1¼ pints) milk
100 g (4 oz) Gruyère cheese, grated
50 g (2 oz) Mozzarella cheese,
grated
3 tbls grated Parmesan cheese
2 tbls fresh white breadcrumbs
sliced grilled tomato, to garnish

Place the water, salt and oil in a large saucepan and bring to the boil.

Add the macaroni to the saucepan, keeping the water boiling. Reduce the heat slightly and cook for 8-10 minutes, stirring occasionally, until macaroni is tender.

Drain the macaroni, rinse with hot water and drain thoroughly in a sieve. Melt a little butter in a saucepan and toss the pasta to coat evenly.

To make the sauce: melt butter or margarine in a pan, adding flour to make a roux. When combined, add milk, Worcestershire sauce, salt, pepper, pinch of cayenne pepper and mustard. Bring to the boil stirring.

Reduce the heat and cook gently for 2-3 minutes. Stir in the macaroni until evenly coated in the sauce.

Mix the three cheeses together and reserve one-third for sprinkling. Add the remaining two-thirds to the sauce, mix well and pour into a buttered ovenproof dish.

Sprinkle the top with the remaining cheese and breadcrumbs.

Place the macaroni cheese under a moderate grill and cook for about 5 minutes until the top is golden brown. Serve immediately garnished with sliced grilled tomato.

You can freeze macaroni cheese before grilling for up to one month. Thaw to room temperature, then reheat in the oven for 20-25 minutes, 190°C, 375°F, Gas Mark 5.

Pasta with meatballs

SERVES 4

50 g (2 oz) fresh white breadcrumbs
2 tbls milk
1 egg, beaten
350 g (12 oz) minced beef
2 garlic cloves, crushed
1 tsp grated lemon rind
25 g (1 oz) grated Parmesan cheese
¼ tsp grated nutmeg
1 tbls chopped fresh parsley
salt and pepper
oil for frying
1½ litres (3 pints) water
1 tsp salt
1 tbls vegetable oil
225 g (8 oz) pasta twists
butter
coriander leaves or fresh parsley, to
garnish
For the sauce:
25 g (1 oz) butter or margarine
175 g (6 oz) button mushrooms,
chopped
2 tbls sherry
142 ml (5 fl oz) carton soured cream

Place the breadcrumbs and milk in a bowl, and leave for 5 minutes. Stir in the egg, minced beef, garlic, lemon rind, Parmesan, nutmeg, parsley and some salt and pepper into the breadcrumb and milk mixture.

Mix together until well blended, then form the mixture into 16 balls. Place on a plate and chill thoroughly for ¾-1 hour.

Heat about 1 cm (½ inch) oil in a frying pan, and add the meatballs.

● Three-cheese macaroni; Pasta with meatballs

Fry for about 5 minutes, turning frequently during the cooking. Drain and keep warm.

Place the water, salt and oil in a large saucepan and bring to the boil.

Add the pasta twists to the saucepan, keeping the water boiling. Reduce the heat slightly and cook the pasta for 8-10 minutes, stirring occasionally, until tender.

Drain the pasta, rinse with hot water and drain thoroughly in a sieve. Melt a little butter in the saucepan and toss the pasta to coat evenly; place in a warmed serving dish and keep warm.

To make the sauce: melt the butter or margarine in a medium saucepan and fry the mushrooms for 2 minutes.

Add the sherry and bring to the boil, then stir in the soured cream and remove from the heat.

Add the meatballs to the sauce and turn gently to coat well.

Arrange the meatballs on top of the pasta and pour over the sauce. Garnish with coriander or parsley.

Beef chow mein

SERVES 4

1 ½ litres (3 pints) water
1 tsp salt
1 tbls vegetable oil
225 g (8 oz) vermicelli
butter
2 tbls sunflower or sesame seed oil
350 g (12 oz) frying steak, cut into
    thin strips
8 spring onions, sliced
1 garlic clove, crushed
1 red pepper, seeded and thinly
    sliced
1 green pepper, seeded and thinly
    sliced
100 g (4 oz) button mushrooms,
    sliced
1 tbls cornflour
2 tbls light soy sauce
2 tbls sherry
150 ml (¼ pint) vegetable or beef
    stock
1 tbls sesame seeds, optional
To garnish:
spring onion tassels (see note)

Place the water, salt and oil in a large saucepan and bring to the boil. Add the vermicelli to the saucepan, keeping the water boiling.

Reduce the heat slightly and cook for 2 minutes if fresh, or according to instructions if packet, stirring occasionally, until the vermicelli is tender.

Drain the vermicelli, rinse with hot water and drain thoroughly in a sieve.

Melt a little butter in the saucepan and toss the vermicelli to coat evenly.

Heat the sunflower or sesame seed oil in a large frying pan, add the steak and fry quickly for 2 minutes.

Remove the meat from the pan using a slotted spoon and place on a plate.

Stir in the onions, garlic, peppers and mushrooms and fry quickly for 1-2 minutes.

Blend together the cornflour, soy sauce and sherry and add to the frying pan with the stock.

Bring to the boil, stirring, and cook for 1 minute. Add the vermicelli and combine with the meat and vegetables.

Arrange the beef chow mein in a warmed serving dish, sprinkle with sesame seeds and garnish with spring onion tassels and pepper rings.

Note: To make spring onion tassels cut the green ends off the onion and slit the remainder in a cross down to the bulb. Place in cold water until the leaves unfurl and form tassels.

Serving idea: Serve with stir-fried vegetables such as bean sprouts.

Lasagne

SERVES 4

1 quantity Bolognese sauce (see page 42).

9 sheets quick-cook egg lasagne
fresh bay leaves, to garnish
For the cheese sauce:
50 g (2 oz) butter or margarine
50 g (2 oz) plain flour
750 ml (1 ¼ pint) milk
½ tsp salt
¼ tsp mustard
cayenne pepper
100 g (4 oz) Cheddar cheese,
    grated
1 egg, beaten

Make the Bolognese sauce according to the recipe on page 42. Heat the oven to 200°C, 400°F, Gas Mark 6.

To make the cheese sauce: melt the butter in a saucepan, add the flour and cook for 1 minute. Gradually add the milk, off the heat, beating all the time.

Bring to the boil and cook for 2 minutes, stirring over a moderate heat. Add the salt, mustard and cayenne and remove from the heat.

Stir in 50 g (2 oz) cheese and the egg and beat well together. Butter a shallow oblong 25 cm by 20 cm (10 inch by 8 inch) ovenproof dish.

Layer the Bolognese sauce, pasta and the cheese sauce to fill the dish, ending with a layer of cheese sauce. Sprinkle the lasagne with the remaining cheese.

Cook in the centre of the oven for 30-35 minutes until the pasta is tender and the top is golden brown. Serve hot garnished with fresh bay leaves.

● Beef chow mein; Lasagne

Vegetable and pasta au gratin

SERVES 4

900 ml (1½ pints) water
1 tsp salt
1 tbls vegetable oil
175 g (6 oz) pasta quills
30 g (1¼ oz) butter or margarine
2 courgettes, sliced
1 carrot, sliced
1 leek, trimmed and sliced
2 sticks celery, sliced
1 small aubergine, sliced
100 g (4 oz) broad beans
100 g (4 oz) breadcrumbs
2 tomatoes, sliced
celery leaves, to garnish
For the sauce:
900 ml (1½ pints) milk
1 bay leaf
1 small onion, chopped
2 cloves
6 peppercorns
pinch of salt
25 g (1 oz) butter or margarine
65 g (2½ oz) plain flour
100 g (4 oz) Cheddar cheese,
  grated

First infuse the milk for the sauce. Place the milk, bay leaf, onion, cloves, peppercorns and some salt in a saucepan. Bring to the boil, turn off the heat and cover the saucepan. Leave until cool, then strain.

Place the water, 1 tsp salt and the oil in a pan and bring to the boil.

Add the pasta to the saucepan, keeping the water boiling. Reduce the heat slightly and cook for 2 minutes if fresh or according to instructions if packet, stirring occasionally, until it is tender.

Drain the pasta, rinse with hot water and drain in a sieve.

Melt 5 g (¼ oz) of the butter in the saucepan and toss the pasta until evenly coated. Place in a bowl.

Melt the remaining 25 g (1 oz) butter or margarine in the saucepan, add the courgettes, carrot, leek, celery, aubergine and broad

beans. Cook gently, stirring occasionally, for 2 minutes, then cover and cook until the vegetables are almost tender, about 15-20 minutes.

Using a slotted spoon, lift the vegetables from the cooking liquor, reserving the liquor, and add to the pasta. Stir well.

Melt the butter for the sauce, add flour to make a roux. Then add infused milk and vegetable liquor. Bring to the boil, stirring. Reduce the heat and cook gently for 2 minutes.

Add two-thirds of the cheese, then stir the sauce into the vegetables and pasta until evenly mixed.

Pour the mixture into a buttered shallow ovenproof dish and sprinkle the top with the remaining cheese and the breadcrumbs, then arrange tomato slices across the top.

Place the dish under a moderately hot grill and cook for 5-8 minutes until golden brown. Garnish with celery leaves.

● **Vegetable and pasta au gratin;**
Seafood and vegetable lasagne

Seafood and vegetable lasagne

SERVES 4

1 quantity Seafood sauce (see
  recipe on page 45)
2 tbls vegetable oil
4 tomatoes, skinned, seeded and
  chopped
2 courgettes, sliced
100 g (4 oz) button mushrooms,
  sliced
1½ litres (3 pints) boiling water
1 tsp salt
9 sheets wholewheat or green
  lasagne
2 tbls fresh white or brown
  breadcrumbs
2 tbls Cheddar cheese, grated

Make the Seafood sauce according to the recipe on page 45. Heat the oven to 200°C, 400°F, Gas Mark 6.

Heat 1 tbls oil in a frying pan, add the tomatoes and courgettes and fry for 3-4 minutes until the mixture begins to thicken. Stir in the mushrooms and remove from the heat.

Place the water, salt and remaining oil in a large saucepan and boil.

Feed the lasagne into the saucepan a sheet at a time, keeping the water boiling. Reduce the heat slightly and cook for 10-12 minutes, stirring occasionally, until the lasagne is almost tender.

Drain the lasagne well, rinse with hot water, then separate the sheets and place on a plate.

Butter a shallow 25 cm by 20 cm (10 inch by 8 inch) ovenproof dish.

Spread one-third of the Seafood sauce over the base of the dish, cover with 3 sheets of lasagne and one-third of the vegetable mixture.

Repeat these layers, and sprinkle the breadcrumbs and cheese on top.

Cook in the centre of the oven for 30-35 minutes until the pasta is tender and the top is browned.

Stuffed pasta with tomato sauce

SERVES 4

½ quantity Fresh tomato sauce
    (see recipe page 42)
1½ litres (3 pints) water
1 tsp salt
1 tbls vegetable oil
12 sheets quick-cook egg
    lasagne
6 slices Parma ham
50 g (2 oz) Mozzarella or St Paulin
    cheese
2 tbls grated Parmesan cheese
sprigs of rosemary, to garnish
For the filling:
25 g (1 oz) butter or margarine
225 g (8 oz) button mushrooms,
    finely chopped
½ tsp chopped fresh rosemary
2 tbls plain flour
2 tbls lemon juice
4 tbls single cream
pepper

Make up the Fresh tomato sauce according to the recipe on page 42 .

Place the water, salt and oil in a large saucepan and bring to the boil.

Feed in a few leaves of lasagne at a time, keeping the water boiling. Reduce the heat and cook for 2-3 minutes.

Take out the lasagne and place separately on a board. Repeat to cook the remaining lasagne.

Place half a slice of ham on each piece of lasagne.

Heat the oven to 190°C, 375°F, Gas Mark 5.

Melt the butter in a small saucepan, add the mushrooms and rosemary and fry quickly for 1 minute. Stir in the flour and cook for 1 minute, then stir in the lemon juice. Remove the pan from the heat.

Stir in the cream and some pepper and divide the mushroom filling between the sheets of lasagne.

Spread the filling evenly over the ham and roll up firmly.

Butter a shallow ovenproof dish and pour in half the tomato sauce. Arrange the lasagne rolls in the dish and pour over the remaining sauce.

Sprinkle with Mozzarella and Parmesan and cover with a piece of buttered foil.

Cook in the centre of the oven for 25-30 minutes until the pasta is tender. Remove the foil after 20 minutes of the cooking time.

Serve hot garnished with sprigs of rosemary.

Serving idea: Serve with green beans and cauliflower florets.

Variations: An alternative filling is chopped, cooked spinach and cream or cottage cheese.

• Chicken pot pie; Stuffed pasta with tomato sauce

Chicken pot pie

SERVES 4

1 ¼ kg (2½ lb) chicken
1.2 litres (2 pints) water
1 chicken stock cube
salt and pepper
1 tbls corn oil
225 g (8 oz) smoked bacon, rinded
  and chopped
1 onion, sliced
butter
450 g (1 lb) fresh tagliatelle
175 g (6 oz) potatoes, thinly sliced
225 g (8 oz) sweetcorn kernels
2 tsp chopped fresh tarragon

Cut the legs, wings and breast of the chicken to make 4 neat joints.

Place the chicken carcass in a large saucepan with the water, stock cube and some salt and pepper.

Bring to the boil, cover the sauce-pan with a lid and simmer very gently for 1 hour. Strain stock into a measuring jug.

Heat the oil in a frying pan, add the bacon, onion and chicken joints and fry quickly to brown evenly. Remove from the heat.

Heat the oven to 180°C, 350°F, Gas Mark 4 and butter a 2.4 litre (4 pint) casserole.

Place half the tagliatelle in the base of the dish and cover with half the potato slices and sweetcorn.

Arrange the chicken joints on top of the potatoes and sprinkle with tarragon, bacon and onion and sweetcorn.

Top with the remaining potato slices and tagliatelle. Pour 600 ml (1 pint) stock over the tagliatelle and cover with a lid or buttered foil.

Cook in the centre of the oven for 1-1¼ hours until chicken and pota-toes are tender.

INDEX